24 Passive Income Ideas

Build Assets not Liabilities

Dennis Snyder

Disclaimer:

It is important to consult with a licensed financial advisor or professional before making any financial decisions. Any information provided in this book is for educational or informational purposes only and should not be construed as financial advice. It is important to do your own research and due diligence before making any decisions related to your finances.

DEDICATION

This book s dedicated to my lovely wife, Vicki. She has put up with my entrepreneur endeavors for all of our 52 years of marriage. Five businesses later we are still happily married and in love with each other.

I. Introduction to Passive Income 101

- Definition of passive income
- Benefits of passive income
- Importance of diversifying income streams

II. Investing for Passive Income

- Dividend stocks
- Index funds
- Real estate investment trusts (REITs)
- Peer-to-peer lending
- Crowdfunding platforms

III. Rental Income for Passive Income

- Rental properties
- Airbnb rentals
- Storage unit rentals
- Parking space rentals

IV. Online Business for Passive Income

- Affiliate marketing
- selling physical products
- Selling digital products
- Dropshipping
- Print-on-demand merchandise
- You tube and Podcasts

V. Creative Endeavors for Passive Income

- Writing e-books
- Creating and selling music
- Selling stock photos
- Licensing artwork or designs

VI. Miscellaneous Ideas for Passive Income

- Investing in vending machines
- Renting out billboards or advertising space
- Investing in solar panels
- Investing in cryptocurrency
- Creating a mobile app

VII. Passive Income Recap

- Recap of passive income ideas
- Importance of taking action and starting small.

Chapter 1

Passive Income 101

A Beginner's Introduction to Generating Money While You Sleep

If we want to achieve financial freedom then we need to learn to build assets and not liabilities. Finding and building passive income will help us to do just that.

Are you tired of working long hours every day just to make ends meet? Do you dream of earning money without having to put in constant effort? If so, then you may be interested in learning about passive income 101.

Passive income is money that you earn without actively working for it. This means that once you set up a passive income stream, you can continue to earn money without having to put in ongoing effort. Unlike active income, which requires you to trade your time and effort for money, passive income allows you to earn money while you sleep, travel, or spend time with your family.

There are many different types of passive income streams, including rental income, dividend income, and online business income. While some passive income streams require an initial investment of time or money, others can be set up with little to no upfront costs. By diversifying your passive income streams, you can create a reliable source of income that can help you achieve financial freedom and independence.

What is Passive Income 101?

If you're interested in earning money without actively working for it, then passive income might be something you want to explore. Passive income is defined as any money earned in a manner that does not require too much effort on your part. This series will cover many of these passive income 101 ideas.

Definition

Passive income is income generated from someone other than an employer or a contractor. It can be generated by earning interest on savings, getting cash back or rewards on a credit card, and more. Passive income streams are often set up with an upfront investment of time, money, or both. However, once the initial work is done, you can earn money without much effort on your part.

Passive Income vs Active Income

Passive income is different from active income, which is income generated from actively working for it. Active income includes wages, salaries, tips, and commissions. You trade your time and effort for a paycheck.

Passive income, on the other hand, allows you to earn money without actively working for it. This means you can potentially earn money while you sleep, travel, or spend time with loved ones.

Passive income can come from a variety of sources, and each source has its own pros and cons. For example, rental properties can provide a steady stream of rental income, but they require upfront investments and ongoing maintenance.

Stocks and bonds can provide investment income, but they come with risks and require research and monitoring. Blogs and content can provide advertising revenue, but they require time and effort to build an audience.

Passive income can be a great way to supplement your income, build wealth, and achieve financial freedom. It's important to remember that earning passive income typically requires an upfront investment of time, money, or both. However, once the initial work is done, you can potentially earn money without much effort on your part.

Benefits of Passive Income

Passive income can provide many benefits to you, including financial freedom, flexibility, and diversification. Let's take a closer look at each of these benefits:

Financial Freedom

One of the primary benefits of passive income is that it can provide you with financial freedom. By generating income without having to actively work for it, you can create a steady stream of revenue that can help you achieve your financial goals.

This can include paying off debt, saving for retirement, or even pursuing your passions and hobbies without worrying about money.

Flexibility

Passive income can also provide you with greater flexibility in your life. By generating income without having to actively work for it, you can create more time for yourself and your loved ones. This can include spending more time with your family, traveling, or pursuing other interests and hobbies.

Diversification

Another benefit of passive income is that it can help you diversify your income streams. By investing in different passive income streams, such as real estate, stocks, or bonds, you can create a more balanced and diversified portfolio. This can help protect you against market fluctuations and other economic uncertainties.

Overall, passive income can provide you with many benefits, including financial freedom, flexibility, and diversification. By investing in passive income streams, you can create a more stable and secure financial future for yourself and your loved ones.

Importance of Diversifying Income Streams

When it comes to passive income, diversification is key. Relying on a single source of passive income can be risky and leave you vulnerable to unexpected changes or disruptions. By diversifying your income streams, you can reduce your financial risk and increase your overall income.

There are many ways to diversify your passive income streams. Some options include:

> •Investing in stocks, mutual funds, or bonds
>
> •Creating digital products such as ebooks, online courses, or templates
>
> •Generating rental income from real estate or Airbnb
>
> •Earning royalties from patents, trademarks, or original works
>
> •Starting a blog or YouTube channel and monetizing through ads or affiliate marketing

By having multiple sources of passive income, you can also benefit from different types of income streams. For example, interest income from CDs or money market accounts may be more stable and predictable, while rental income or stock dividends may provide higher returns but come with more risk.

Diversifying your income streams can also help you achieve your financial goals faster. By earning additional income, you can save more money, pay off debt, or invest in new opportunities.

Ultimately, diversifying your passive income streams can provide you with greater financial security and freedom. By creating a portfolio of income streams, you can enjoy the benefits of passive income while minimizing your risks and maximizing your earning potential.

Common Misconceptions About Passive Income

If you're new to the world of passive income, you may have heard some misconceptions about it. Here are a few common ones:

1. Passive income is easy money.

While it's true that passive income can provide a steady stream of income without much ongoing effort, it's not necessarily easy money.

You'll still need to put in some work upfront to set up your passive income streams, and you may need to make adjustments along the way to ensure they continue to generate income.

2. Passive income requires no investment.

While there are some passive income streams that require little to no investment, such as affiliate marketing or selling digital products, many others do require an initial investment. For example, if you want to generate passive income through rental properties, you'll need to invest in real estate.

3. Passive income is completely hands-off.

While passive income can provide a more hands-off approach to generating income compared to traditional jobs, it's not completely hands-off. You'll still need to monitor your passive income streams to ensure they're generating income and make adjustments as needed.

4. Passive income is a get-rich-quick scheme.

Passive income can provide a steady stream of income over time, but it's not a get-rich-quick scheme. It takes time and effort to set up your passive income streams, and it may take some time before you see a significant return on your investment.

5. Passive income is only for the wealthy.

While some passive income streams may require a significant investment upfront, there are many others that can be started with little to no money. For example, you can start a blog or YouTube channel with just a computer and an internet connection.

By understanding these common misconceptions, you'll be better equipped to pursue passive income streams that align with your goals and expectations.

Passive Income 101 Conclusion

Passive income is a great way to earn money without having to continuously work for it. By investing your time and money into creating passive income streams, you can generate a steady flow of income that can help you achieve your financial goals.

Remember, creating passive income streams requires effort and upfront capital. You need to be willing to put in the work upfront to reap the benefits later on. But once you have established your passive income streams, you can sit back and watch the money roll in.

There are many different ways to create passive income streams, from investing in stocks and real estate to creating digital products and selling them online. The key is to find a strategy that works for you and your financial goals.

Don't be afraid to experiment with different passive income strategies until you find the ones that work best for you. And remember, it's important to diversify your passive income streams to minimize risk and ensure a steady flow of income.

So, start exploring your options and take action today to create your own passive income streams. With dedication and hard work, you can achieve financial freedom and live the life you've always dreamed of. Once I learned that we need to build assets and not liabiities, the lid blew off.

CHAPTER 2

Investing for Passive Income

If you're looking to generate passive income, investing for passive income is one of the most effective ways to do it. By investing your money in assets that generate income, you can earn money without having to actively work for it. Passive income is money that you earn without having to put in any additional effort once you've made your initial investment.

Of course, investing always carries some level of risk, and it's important to do your research and understand the potential risks and rewards before making any investment decisions.

However, by investing wisely and diversifying your portfolio, you can create a reliable source of passive income that can help you achieve your financial goals.

Investing for Passive Income Strategies

Investing for passive income involves putting your money into various investments that can generate income without requiring your active involvement. Here are some strategies for investing in passive income:

Stocks

Investing in stocks is a popular way to generate passive income.

When you buy stocks, you become a part owner of the company and can earn dividends when the company distributes part of its earnings to shareholders. Dividend-paying stocks are a good option for investors looking for a steady income stream. However, keep in mind that stocks can be volatile and their value can fluctuate based on market conditions.

Index Funds

Index funds are a type of mutual fund that tracks a specific market index, such as the S&P 500. They offer a diversified portfolio of stocks with low fees and can be a good option for passive investors who want exposure to the stock market without the risk of active management. Index funds can provide a steady income stream through dividends and capital gains.

REITs

Real estate investment trusts (REITs) are companies that own and manage income-producing real estate properties, such as rental properties, commercial buildings, and hotels. Investing in REITs can provide a steady income stream through rental income and can offer diversification in a portfolio. However, keep in mind that REITs can be subject to market fluctuations and may have high fees.

Peer-to-Peer Lending

Peer-to-peer lending platforms, such as Prosper and Lending Club, allow investors to lend money to individuals or businesses in exchange for interest income. This can be a good option for investors looking for higher returns than savings accounts or CDs. However, keep in mind that peer-to-peer lending can be risky and may not be suitable for all investors.

Crowdfunding Platforms

Crowdfunding platforms, such as Fundrise, allow investors to pool their money together to invest in real estate projects. This can provide a steady income stream through rental income and can offer diversification in a portfolio. However, keep in mind that crowdfunding investments can be illiquid and may have high fees.

Investing for Passive Income Risks

While investing in passive income streams can provide a steady source of income, it is important to understand the potential risks involved. In this section, we will discuss two major risks associated with passive income: market volatility and tax implications.

Market Volatility

One of the biggest risks associated with passive income is market volatility. The value of your investments can rise and fall with the market, which can impact your overall returns. This is particularly true for stocks and shares, which can be affected by a range of factors including economic conditions, company performance, and global events.

It is important to remember that while market volatility can be unsettling, it is also a natural part of investing. By diversifying your portfolio and investing in a range of different assets, you can help to mitigate the impact of market fluctuations on your passive income streams.

Tax Implications

Another important factor to consider when investing in passive income streams is the tax implications. Depending on the type of investment, you may be required to pay taxes on your dividends or profits.

For example, if you invest in stocks that pay dividends, these dividends may be subject to income tax. Similarly, if you invest in a rental property, you will need to pay taxes on the rental income you receive.

It is important to consult with a financial advisor or tax professional to understand the tax implications of your passive income investments. They can help you to identify potential tax deductions and ensure that you are meeting all of your tax obligations.

Passive Income Maintenance

Investing for passive income requires ongoing maintenance to ensure your portfolio continues to generate income. Here are some key maintenance tasks to keep your portfolio on track:

Expense Ratios

Expense ratios are the fees charged by mutual funds and exchange-traded funds (ETFs) to cover their operating costs. These fees can eat into your returns over time, so it's important to keep an eye on them. Look for low-cost funds with expense ratios under 0.5%, and avoid funds with expense ratios over 1%.

Rebalancing

Rebalancing involves periodically adjusting your portfolio to maintain your desired asset allocation. For example, if your target allocation is 60% stocks and 40% bonds, and stocks have performed well recently, your portfolio may now be 70% stocks and 30% bonds. Rebalancing would involve selling some stocks and buying some bonds to get back to your target allocation. Rebalancing can help manage risk and ensure your portfolio stays aligned with your goals.

Monitoring

Monitoring your portfolio regularly is important to ensure it continues to meet your needs. Keep an eye on your investments to make sure they are performing as expected, and adjust your portfolio if your goals or circumstances change. Be prepared to weather market downturns, and resist the urge to make impulsive decisions based on short-term market movements.

By following these maintenance tasks, you can help ensure your portfolio generates passive income over the long term.

Working with a Financial Advisor

Investing for passive income can be a great way to generate a steady stream of money with minimal effort. However, it can be challenging to determine the best investment strategies and identify the right opportunities. That's where a financial advisor can come in handy. A financial advisor can help you navigate the complex world of securities and find the best passive income opportunities that suit your needs and goals.

Robo-Advisors

Robo-advisors are automated investment platforms that use algorithms to manage your portfolio. They offer a low-cost alternative to traditional financial advisors and can be a great option if you're just starting out with passive income investing. Robo-advisors typically charge lower fees and require lower minimum investments than traditional advisors. However, they may not offer the same level of personalized advice and guidance as human advisors.

Active Management

Active management involves hiring a professional fund manager to actively manage your investments. This can be a good option if you're looking for a more hands-on approach to passive income investing. Active managers can help you identify the best investment opportunities and adjust your portfolio as market conditions change. However, active management can be expensive and may not always yield better returns than passive strategies.

Limited Partners

Limited partnerships are investment vehicles that allow investors to pool their money together to invest in a specific project or venture. Limited partners are typically passive investors who provide funding but have limited control over the project. Limited partnerships can be a good option if you're looking for a more hands-off approach to passive income investing. However, limited partnerships can be risky and may require a significant upfront investment.

Accredited Investors

Accredited investors are individuals or institutions that meet certain financial criteria and are allowed to invest in private securities offerings. Accredited investors typically have a higher net worth and are considered to be more sophisticated investors. Investing in private securities offerings can be a good way to generate passive income, but it can also be risky and may require a significant upfront investment. If you're considering investing in private securities offerings, it's important to work with a financial advisor who has experience in this area.

Investing for Passive Income Conclusion

Congratulations! You have learned about various ways to invest for passive income. By investing in dividend-paying stocks or funds like Dividend Aristocrats, you can earn a steady stream of income without having to do much work. Just remember to diversify your portfolio and choose stocks or funds with a high dividend yield to maximize your returns.

For those looking to earn interest income, high-yield savings accounts or peer-to-peer lending platforms like Lending Club can be good options. However, keep in mind that these options come with some risk and may not provide the same returns as other investments.

It's also important to consider tax benefits when investing for passive income. Retirement accounts like a 401(k) or IRA can provide significant tax benefits, making them a great option for long-term investing.

Overall, investing for passive income requires careful consideration and research. Choose investments that align with your financial goals and risk tolerance, and remember to diversify your portfolio to minimize risk.

CHAPTER 3

Rental Income for Passive Income

How to Generate Reliable Cash Flow

If you're looking for a way to earn extra income without having to work more hours or put in more effort, rental income for passive income can be a great option.

Rental income is a form of passive income, which means you earn money without actively working for it. This can be a great way to supplement your regular income, save for retirement, or even achieve financial independence.

Passive income can come from a variety of sources, including rental properties, investments, and businesses. However, rental income is one of the most popular forms of passive income, especially for those who are just starting out.

With rental income, you can earn money by renting out a property you own, such as a house, apartment, or commercial space. This can provide a steady stream of income that requires little to no effort on your part.

Of course, earning rental income isn't as simple as buying a property and waiting for the money to roll in. There are many factors to consider, such as location, property type, and tenant screening.

Additionally, there are tax implications to consider, as rental income is subject to taxes. However, with the right approach and a little bit of knowledge, rental income can be a great way to earn passive income and achieve your financial goals.

What is Rental Income?

If you are looking for a way to generate passive income, rental income is a popular option to consider. Rental income is the money you earn from renting out a property to tenants. This can include both residential and commercial properties, such as apartments, houses, office spaces, and retail stores.

Definition

According to the IRS, rental income is defined as "any payment you receive for the use or occupation of property." This can include rent payments, security deposits, and any other fees related to the rental of the property. Rental income can be further classified as either gross rental income or net rental income.

Gross rental income is the total amount of rental income you receive before deducting any expenses. Net rental income, on the other hand, is the amount of rental income you have left after deducting expenses such as property taxes, mortgage payments, insurance, and maintenance costs.

It is important to note that rental income is considered passive income by the IRS, which means it is not subject to self-employment taxes. This can make rental income an attractive option for those looking to generate passive income.

When it comes to rental properties, there are a few things to keep in mind. First, it is important to find the right tenants for your property. This can involve conducting background checks, verifying employment and income, and checking references. It is also important to set a fair rental price that reflects the market value of the property.

Additionally, it is important to maintain the property to ensure it remains attractive to tenants. This can include regular maintenance and repairs, as well as upgrades and renovations as needed.

Overall, rental income can be a great way to generate passive income, but it does require some effort and investment on your part. By finding the right property, setting a fair rental price, and maintaining the property, you can generate a steady stream of rental income over time.

Types of Rental Income

When it comes to passive income, rental properties are a popular choice. There are several types of rental income that you can earn, each with its own advantages and disadvantages.

Rental properties

Rental properties are a traditional way of earning rental income. You can buy a property and rent it out to tenants. This can be a single-family home, a duplex, or even an apartment complex.

The advantage of rental properties is that they can provide a steady stream of income. However, there are also some disadvantages. You are responsible for maintaining the property and finding tenants. If the property is vacant, you won't earn any income.

Airbnb rentals

Airbnb rentals are becoming increasingly popular. With Airbnb, you can rent out a room in your home or your entire home to travelers. The advantage of Airbnb rentals is that you can earn more money than with traditional rentals.

However, there are also some disadvantages. You need to be available to check in guests and provide a clean and comfortable space for them. You also need to be aware of local laws and regulations regarding short-term rentals.

Storage unit rentals

Storage unit rentals are another option for earning rental income. You can buy or rent a storage unit and rent it out to people who need extra space to store their belongings. The advantage of storage unit rentals is that they require less maintenance than rental properties.

However, there are also some disadvantages. You need to find a location that is convenient for renters, and you need to be aware of any zoning laws or regulations that may apply.

Parking space rentals

Parking space rentals are a simple way of earning rental income. You can rent out a parking space in your driveway or garage to someone who needs a place to park their car. The advantage of parking space rentals is that they require very little maintenance.

However, there are also some disadvantages. You need to find a location that is convenient for renters, and you need to be aware of any zoning laws or regulations that may apply.

Benefits of Rental Income

Investing in rental properties can provide various benefits, including passive income, steady cash flow, and tax benefits.

Passive Income

One of the primary benefits of rental income is that it can be a source of passive income. Passive income is money earned without actively working for it.

Owning rental property can be a great way to generate passive income because you can earn money from rent payments without having to put in significant effort or time.

Steady Cash Flow

Rental income can provide a steady cash flow that can help cover your expenses and provide financial stability. When you have tenants paying rent each month, you have a reliable source of income that can help you pay off debt, save for retirement, or invest in other opportunities.

Tax Benefits

Investing in rental properties can also provide tax benefits. The IRS allows you to deduct certain expenses related to your rental property, such as mortgage interest, property taxes, and operating expenses.

Additionally, you may be able to depreciate the value of your rental property over time, which can help reduce your taxable income.

It's important to note that the tax treatment of rental income can depend on various factors, including your level of involvement in managing the property and your income level. Consult a tax professional to ensure you are taking advantage of all the tax benefits available to you.

Overall, rental income can be a valuable investment opportunity that can provide passive income, steady cash flow, and tax benefits.

Whether you're looking to diversify your investment portfolio or generate additional income, rental properties may be worth considering.

Risks and Challenges of Rental Income

While rental income can be a great source of passive income, it's not without its risks and challenges. Here are some potential issues to be aware of:

Maintenance and Repairs

As a landlord, you are responsible for maintaining your rental property. This includes fixing any issues that arise, such as leaky faucets or broken appliances. Depending on the age and condition of the property, these costs can add up quickly.

It's important to budget for regular maintenance and repairs to ensure that your property stays in good condition and your tenants are happy.

Vacancies and Tenant Issues

One of the biggest risks of rental income for passive income are vacancies. If your property sits empty for an extended period of time, you'll lose out on rental income and may struggle to cover your mortgage payments.

Additionally, dealing with difficult tenants can be a headache. From late rent payments to property damage, tenant issues can quickly become a drain on your time and resources.

Market Fluctuations

The value of your rental property can fluctuate based on a variety of factors, including location, job growth, and market conditions. If you've taken on debt to purchase your rental property, a downturn in the market can make it difficult to cover your mortgage payments.

Additionally, if you rely on rental income to cover your expenses, a dip in the market could lead to financial hardship.

Overall, rental income can be a great way to generate passive income, but it's important to be aware of the risks and challenges involved. By budgeting for maintenance and repairs, carefully screening tenants, and staying up-to-date on market conditions, you can minimize your risks and enjoy steady rental income for years to come.

Tips for Maximizing Rental Income

Maximizing rental income for passive income is a key goal for any landlord or property owner. Here are some tips to help you increase your rental income:

Effective Property Management

Effective property management is crucial for maximizing rental income. Here are some tips:

- Screen tenants carefully to ensure they are reliable and will pay rent on time.

- Respond to tenant complaints and maintenance requests promptly to keep tenants satisfied and prevent small problems from turning into big ones.

- Regularly inspect your property to identify any maintenance or repair needs before they become major issues.

Location and Market Analysis

The location of your rental property can have a big impact on its rental income potential. Here are some tips:

- Research the local rental market to determine what similar properties are renting for.

- Consider the neighborhood and proximity to amenities like schools, parks, and public transportation when setting rental rates.

- Stay up-to-date on local development and economic trends that could affect your property's value and rental income potential.

Maintenance and Repairs

Maintaining your rental property and making necessary repairs can help you maximize rental income by attracting and retaining reliable tenants. Here are some tips:

- •Regularly clean and maintain your property to keep it in good condition and prevent larger repair needs from arising.

- •Make necessary repairs promptly to prevent further damage and keep tenants satisfied.

- •Consider upgrading your property with amenities like new appliances or updated finishes to attract higher-paying tenants.

Rental Income for Passive Income Conclusion

Overall, rental income can be an excellent way to generate passive income. However, it is important to understand the tax implications and the level of involvement required to make it truly passive.

Remember to keep accurate records of expenses and income, and consult with a tax professional to ensure you are taking advantage of any available deductions.

Consider investing in a property management company to take care of the day-to-day operations and maintenance of your rental property. This can free up your time and allow you to truly enjoy the passive income that rental properties can provide.

Additionally, be sure to carefully research the location and type of property you are investing in to ensure it has a good potential for rental income. Look for areas with low vacancy rates and high demand for rental properties.

Finally, remember that rental income is just one of many ways to generate passive income. Consider diversifying your portfolio with other passive income streams such as dividend stocks, peer-to-peer lending, or creating digital products.

CHAPTER 4

Online Business for Passive Income

How to Build a Profitable Stream of Passive Revenue

If you're looking for ways to earn extra money without putting in a lot of effort, starting an online business for passive income might be the perfect solution for you. Passive income is money earned with little to no effort on your part, and an online business can be a great way to generate it.

There are many different types of online businesses that can generate passive income, including dropshipping stores, print-on-demand shops, and affiliate marketing websites.

With a dropshipping store, you can sell products without ever having to handle inventory or shipping.

A print-on-demand shop lets you sell custom-designed products without having to worry about printing or shipping them yourself.

And with an affiliate marketing website, you can earn commissions by promoting other people's products.

Starting an online business for passive income can be a great way to supplement your income, or even replace your full-time job. While it may take some effort to get started, once your business is up and running, you can sit back and watch the money roll in.

So if you're looking for a way to earn extra income without a lot of work, starting an online business for passive income might be the perfect solution for you.

Types of Passive Income

If you're looking for ways to earn passive income, there are several options available. Here are some of the most popular types of online business for passive income:

Affiliate Marketing

Affiliate marketing involves promoting other people's products or services and earning a commission for each sale made through your unique affiliate link. This can be done through a blog, social media, or other online platforms.

It's a popular way to earn passive income, but it requires time and effort to build an audience and establish trust with your followers.

Dropshipping

Dropshipping is a business model that allows you to sell products without holding any inventory. You partner with a supplier who handles the shipping and fulfillment, and you earn a profit on each sale.

This can be a great way to start an online business with minimal investment, but it requires careful product selection and marketing strategies to be successful.

Selling Physical Products

If you have a product idea, you can sell physical products online through marketplaces like Amazon or your own e-commerce store. This can be a lucrative way to earn passive income, but it requires investment in inventory and fulfillment logistics.

Digital Products

Digital products like e-books, courses, and software can be created once and sold multiple times, making them a great source of passive income. However, it requires knowledge and skills to create high-quality digital products that people are willing to pay for.

Print-on-demand Merchandise

Print-on-demand merchandise allows you to sell custom-designed products like t-shirts, mugs, and phone cases without holding any inventory. You partner with a supplier who prints and ships the products, and you earn a profit on each sale.

This can be a low-risk way to start an online business, but it requires careful product selection and marketing strategies to be successful.

YouTube and Podcasts

Creating content on platforms like YouTube and podcasts can earn you passive income through advertising revenue, sponsorships, and affiliate links.

However, it requires time and effort to build an audience and create high-quality content that people want to consume.

These are just a few examples of the many types of passive income available. Each option has its own pros and cons, and it's important to choose one that aligns with your interests, skills, and financial goals.

Tips for Building a Successful Online Business for Passive Income

Building a successful online business for passive income takes time and effort, but the rewards can be significant. Here are some tips to help you create a profitable online business that generates passive income:

Identifying Your Target Audience

The first step in building a successful online business is to identify your target audience. Knowing who your audience is will help you create content that resonates with them and drives traffic to your website.

Use tools like Google Analytics to gather data about your audience, including their age, gender, location, and interests. This information will help you tailor your content to meet their needs and preferences.

Creating High-Quality Content

Creating high-quality content is essential for building a successful online business. Your content should be informative, engaging, and relevant to your target audience. Use a mix of text, images, and videos to keep your audience engaged and interested.

Make sure your content is optimized for search engines by using relevant keywords and meta descriptions.

Building an Online Presence

Building an online presence is key to driving traffic to your website and building a loyal following. Use social media platforms like Facebook, Twitter, and Instagram to promote your content and engage with your audience.

Join online communities and forums related to your niche to connect with other entrepreneurs and potential customers.

Monetizing Your Content

There are many ways to monetize your content and generate passive income from your online business. Some popular options include affiliate marketing, sponsored content, and selling digital products like e-books and online courses.

You can also generate passive income through advertising revenue, such as display ads or Google AdSense. Consider diversifying your income streams by investing in stocks or real estate, or creating a mobile app or dropshipping business.

Remember, building a successful online business takes time and effort. Stay focused on your goals and be patient as you build your audience and generate passive income.

With the right strategies and a little bit of luck, you can create a profitable online business for passive income that provides financial security and the freedom to live life on your own terms.

Online Business for Passive Income Conclusion

Congratulations! You have learned about various online business models that can help you earn passive income. Remember, passive income requires effort and time upfront, but it can provide a steady stream of income in the long run.

When choosing an online business, consider your interests, skills, and available resources. It's also important to research and understand the market demand, competition, and potential profitability of your chosen niche.

Dropshipping, blogging, online courses, print-on-demand, and affiliate marketing are some of the popular online business models for passive income.

However, there are many other options available, such as creating and selling digital products, investing in stocks or cryptocurrency, or buying and renting out websites.

Remember to diversify your income streams and continuously learn and adapt to the changing market trends and consumer behavior. Building a successful online business for passive income requires patience, perseverance, and a growth mindset.

So, what are you waiting for? Start exploring and experimenting with different online business models and take the first step towards financial freedom and flexibility. Good luck!

CHAPTER 5

Creative Endeavors for Passive Income

Exploring Profitable Hobbies for Passive income

If you're looking for ways to earn extra money without actively working for it, then passive income may be the answer. Passive income refers to money earned from investments or business ventures that require little to no effort to maintain.

It's a great way to achieve financial freedom and earn money while pursuing your creative endeavors.

One of the best ways to generate passive income is by pursuing your creative passions. Whether you're an artist, musician, writer, or photographer, there are plenty of opportunities to turn your hobbies into a source of income.

By creating and selling your art, music, writing, or photography online, you can earn money while doing something you love.

There are many creative endeavors that can be turned into passive income streams. For example, you can sell your artwork on sites like Etsy or Redbubble, create and sell digital products like e-books or courses, or license your music or photography for commercial use.

With a little creativity and effort, you can turn your passion into a lucrative source of passive income.

Books and E-books

If you're looking to create passive income through creative endeavors, writing and selling books and e-books can be a great option. With the rise of digital publishing, it's easier than ever to self-publish your work and start earning money from it.

Creating Digital Products

One way to create passive income through books and e-books is by creating digital products. This can include online courses, templates, and other resources that people can purchase and download.

I actually have a number of books and e-books on Amazon that sell from time to time. You can check them out here at Concerning Life Publishing.

By creating digital products, you can earn money from your work without having to worry about printing, shipping, or other logistical issues.

When creating digital products, you'll want to make sure that they are high-quality and provide real value to your customers.

Consider creating online courses that teach a specific skill or offer a unique perspective on a topic. You can also create templates for things like resumes, business plans, or social media graphics.

Selling Digital Products

Once you've created your digital products, you'll need to find a way to sell them online. There are a number of platforms that allow you to sell digital products, including your own website, online marketplaces like Etsy or Creative Market, and e-commerce platforms like Gumroad or SendOwl.

When selling digital products, it's important to promote them effectively. Consider using affiliate marketing or affiliate links to drive traffic to your products. You can also use social media and email marketing to reach potential customers.

Licensing and Selling E-books

In addition to creating digital products, you can also earn passive income by licensing and selling e-books. This can include fiction or non-fiction books, as well as educational materials like textbooks or study guides.

When licensing your e-books, you'll want to make sure that you retain the rights to your work and that you're getting a fair share of the profits. You can also sell your e-books directly through platforms like Amazon Kindle Direct Publishing or Apple iBooks.

Overall, creating and selling books and e-books can be a great way to earn passive income through creative endeavors.

By creating high-quality digital products and promoting them effectively, you can build a sustainable income stream that allows you to share your knowledge and expertise with others.

Selling Stock Photos

If you're passionate about photography and enjoy taking pictures, you can turn your hobby into a source of passive income by selling your photos online.

There are several stock photography websites where you can upload your images and earn money every time someone downloads them.

Before you start selling your photos, it's important to understand what types of images sell well in the stock photography market.

Popular categories include nature, travel, food, and lifestyle. It's also important to make sure your photos are high-quality and have good composition.

When it comes to pricing, different stock photography websites have different payment structures. Some websites pay a flat fee per image, while others pay a percentage of the sale. It's important to research and compare different websites to find the best fit for you.

One important thing to keep in mind is that selling stock photos is a competitive market, so it's important to have a large portfolio of high-quality images to increase your chances of making sales.

You can also consider offering exclusive images through certain websites to increase your earnings.

Overall, selling stock photos can be a great way to earn passive income from your photography hobby. With some research and effort, you can turn your passion into a profitable side hustle.

Creating and Selling Music

If you have a passion for music and some skills in creating it, you can turn your hobby into a source of passive income. The music industry is constantly in need of new and fresh sounds, and there are many ways to monetize your creations. Here are some ideas:

 •Licensing your music: You can earn passive income by licensing your music to TV shows, movies, commercials, and other media. Platforms like Audio Network, Pond5, and Songtradr allow you to upload your music and make it available for licensing. Make sure to create music that is commercially viable and fits the needs of the media you are targeting.

 •Selling your music online: You can sell your music directly to consumers through online marketplaces like Bandcamp, Beatstars, and Tunecore. You can also sell your music on platforms like Amazon and iTunes. Make sure to promote your music on social media and other channels to reach a wider audience.

 •Creating music for content creators: You can create music for content creators on platforms like Epidemic Soundand Artlist. These platforms allow content creators to access a library of music and sound effects for their videos. You can earn passive income by creating music that fits the needs of these creators.

Keep in mind that creating and selling music requires some investment in equipment and software. You will also need to spend time promoting your music and building your brand.

However, if you have a talent for creating music and are willing to put in the effort, you can turn your passion into a lucrative source of passive income.

Licensing Artwork or Designs

If you're an artist or designer, you can earn passive income by licensing your artwork or designs. Licensing your work means that you give someone else the right to use your work in exchange for a fee or royalty.

This can be a great way to earn money from your art without having to physically create and sell each piece.

One way to license your artwork is through art licensing agencies.

These agencies work as a middleman between you and potential clients. They will promote your work to companies looking for art to use on their products, such as greeting cards, home decor, and apparel. Some popular art licensing agencies include Tiphaine and Wild Apple.

Another option is to license your designs directly to companies. You can reach out to companies that you think would be a good fit for your work and pitch your designs to them.

This can be a bit more challenging than working with an agency, but it can also be more lucrative since you won't have to split your earnings with a middleman.

Before you start licensing your artwork or designs, it's important to understand the legal aspects of licensing. You'll need to create a licensing agreement that outlines the terms of the license, such as the duration of the license, the fee or royalty you'll receive, and how the artwork can be used.

It's a good idea to work with a lawyer to create a solid licensing agreement that protects your rights as an artist.

Keep in mind that licensing your artwork or designs can be a competitive field, so it's important to have a strong portfolio and be persistent in your efforts. With the right approach, licensing your work can be a great way to earn passive income from your creative endeavors.

Creative Endeavors for Passive Income Conclusion

In conclusion, pursuing creative endeavors for passive income can be a great way to supplement your active income or start a side hustle. With the right business model, you can generate residual income while maintaining flexibility in your schedule.

Whether you're an artist, musician, writer, or designer, there are many ways to monetize your creative skills. From selling digital products like e-books or music downloads to creating and selling online courses, the opportunities are endless.

One of the biggest advantages of pursuing creative endeavors for passive income is the potential for financial freedom. By investing time and effort upfront, you can create a stream of income that continues to generate revenue long after the initial work is done.

However, it's important to keep in mind that starting a creative passive income stream may require some startup capital.

For example, if you want to create and sell physical products like art prints or merchandise, you may need to invest in materials and equipment.

Overall, pursuing creative endeavors for passive income can be a rewarding and lucrative venture. With the right mindset and business model, you can turn your passion into profit and achieve financial freedom.

CHAPTER 6

Miscellaneous Ideas for Passive Income

How to Boost Your Earnings Passively

In this chapter, we'll explore some miscellaneous ideas for passive income that you can consider, some of which may be a good fit for your financial goals and lifestyle.

If you're looking to increase your income without putting in a lot of extra time or effort, passive income streams can be a great solution.

Passive income is money that you earn without actively working for it, usually through investments or other sources that require little ongoing effort on your part.

One popular option for passive income is investing in stocks. While there is always some risk involved with investing, stocks can provide a relatively stable source of passive income over time. By buying shares in companies that pay dividends, you can earn a regular income without having to actively manage your investments.

Of course, it's important to do your research and choose stocks that are likely to perform well over the long term, and to diversify your portfolio to minimize risk.

Another way to generate passive income is to invest in real estate.

This can involve buying rental properties or investing in real estate investment trusts (REITs), which allow you to invest in real estate without having to manage properties yourself.

Real estate can be a great source of passive income, but it does require a significant upfront investment and ongoing management, so it may not be the best option for everyone.

Miscellaneous Ideas for Passive Income

Passive income is a great way to earn money without having to actively work for it. If you're looking for some miscellaneous ideas for passive income, here are a few options to consider:

Vending Machines

Investing in vending machines can be a lucrative way to earn passive income. You can buy or rent vending machines and place them in high-traffic areas such as malls, schools, and office buildings.

You can offer a variety of products such as snacks, drinks, and even electronics. Once you've placed the machines, you'll earn money every time someone makes a purchase.

Renting out Billboards or Advertising Space

If you own a property that's located in a high-traffic area, you can rent out billboards or advertising space to businesses. This is a great way to earn passive income because you don't have to actively manage the advertisements. You can simply collect the rent every month.

Investing in Solar Panels

Investing in solar panels is a great way to earn passive income while also doing something good for the environment. You can install solar panels on your property and sell the excess energy back to the grid. This can be a great way to earn money while also reducing your energy bill.

Mobile Apps

If you have an idea for a mobile app, you can develop it and earn passive income through in-app purchases, ads, and subscriptions. You can also consider buying an existing app or investing in an app development company.

Cryptocurrencies

Investing in cryptocurrencies such as Bitcoin, Ethereum, and Litecoin can be a great way to earn passive income. You can buy and hold these currencies and earn money as their value increases over time.

However, it's important to remember that cryptocurrencies can be volatile, so it's important to do your research and invest wisely.

These are just a few miscellaneous ideas for earning passive income. Whether you're interested in vending machines, solar panels, or mobile apps, there are plenty of options to consider.

By investing in passive income streams, you can earn money while also having more free time to pursue other interests.

Miscellaneous Ideas for Passive Income Conclusion

Congratulations! You are now equipped with a variety of passive income ideas that can help you achieve financial independence and freedom.

Remember, the key to building a successful passive income stream is to choose a source of income that aligns with your interests, skills, and financial goals.

Whether you decide to invest in peer lending, create a mobile app, or invest in renewable energy, it's important to do your research and seek the advice of a financial advisor if needed.

Recurring income sources such as rental properties, dividend-paying stocks, and online courses can also provide a steady stream of passive income over time.

Don't forget about the potential of cryptocurrencies and robo-advisors for passive income generation. Just be sure to approach these options with caution and do your due diligence before investing any real money.

Overall, building a successful passive income stream takes time, effort, and patience. But with the right approach and mindset, you can create a reliable source of income that can help you achieve your financial goals and live the life you've always wanted.

CHAPTER 7

Passive Income 101 Recap

A Comprehensive Review of Earnings through Minimal Effort

If you're looking to generate income without having to work actively for it, then passive income is the way to go. Passive income is money earned from investments, rental properties, or other ventures in which you're not actively involved.

The beauty of passive income is that once you set it up, it can generate income for you without requiring much effort on your part.

There are a variety of passive income streams to choose from, each with its own pros and cons. For example, investing in stocks or bonds can be a great way to generate passive income, but it can also be risky.

Rental properties can provide a steady stream of income, but they require a significant upfront investment and ongoing maintenance.

Creating and selling digital products, such as online courses or ebooks, can be a low-cost way to generate passive income, but it requires time and effort to create the product.

There are many more miscellaneous passive income ideas all around us. And a lot of Creative Endeavors for Passive Income.

Passive income can be a great way to supplement your income, build wealth, or achieve financial independence. However, it's important to do your research and choose the right passive income stream for you.

In this article, we'll provide a recap of some of the most popular passive income streams, their pros and cons, and how to get started with each. Whether you're a beginner or an experienced investor, this article will provide valuable insights into generating passive income.

Recap of Passive Income Ideas

Passive income is a great way to create an additional income stream without having to actively work for it. In contrast to active income, passive income is unearned income that requires little to no effort to maintain.

In this section, we will recap some of the best passive income ideas that we have covered so far.

One of the most popular passive income ideas is investing. Investing your money in stocks, bonds, or real estate can generate significant returns over time. Dividend stocks are a great option for generating passive income as they pay out a portion of the company's profits to shareholders.

Real estate can also be a great investment as rental income can provide a steady stream of passive income.

Another popular passive income idea is creating and selling digital products. This includes creating online courses, eBooks, and printables. These products can be sold on platforms like Udemy, Amazon, or Etsy.

Once you have created the product, you can continue to earn money from it without having to put in any additional effort.

Dropshipping is another popular passive income idea. This involves creating an online store and selling products without having to hold inventory. When a customer places an order, the product is shipped directly from the supplier to the customer. This eliminates the need for you to hold inventory or handle shipping.

Affiliate marketing is also a great way to generate passive income. This involves promoting other people's products and earning a commission on any sales made through your unique affiliate link. You can promote products through your blog, social media, or email marketing campaigns.

Finally, rental income is another great way to generate passive income. This can include renting out a spare room in your home on Airbnb, renting out a storage space, or even renting out your car through platforms like Turo.

Overall, there are many different passive income ideas to choose from. Whether you are looking to invest your money, create digital products, or rent out your assets, there is a passive income idea that can work for you.

By diversifying your income streams and investing in passive income, you can create a more stable financial future for yourself.

Avoiding Passive Income Scams

Common Passive Income Scams

Passive income can be an attractive way to earn money, but there are several common scams you should be aware of:

- •Ponzi schemes: With a Ponzi scheme, a scammer may promise you large returns on your investment but is ultimately out to steal your money. These scammers use part of your investment to pay earlier investors and keep the rest for themselves.
- •Pyramid schemes: In a pyramid scheme, you are asked to invest money in exchange for the promise of future payments. The only way to make money is by recruiting more people to invest, and eventually, the scheme will collapse.
- •Multi-level marketing (MLM) schemes: MLMs are similar to pyramid schemes, but they involve selling products or services. However, the focus is still on recruiting new members rather than selling products.

How to Avoid Passive Income Scams

Here are some tips to help you avoid falling victim to a passive income scam:

- •Do your research: Before investing in any passive income opportunity, do your due diligence. Research the company or individual offering the opportunity, and look for reviews or complaints online.

•Be wary of promises of easy money: If an opportunity sounds too good to be true, it probably is. Be skeptical of anyone who promises you easy money with little effort.

•Don't invest more than you can afford to lose: Never invest money that you can't afford to lose. If you do decide to invest, start with a small amount and see how it goes before investing more.

•Be cautious of influencers: Many influencers promote passive income opportunities, but they may not have your best interests in mind. They may be getting paid to promote a scam, so be cautious of any recommendations they make.

•Be careful with crowdfunding: Crowdfunding can be a great way to raise money for a project, but it's important to be careful. Make sure the project is legitimate and that the people behind it are trustworthy.

•Be cautious of dropshipping: Dropshipping can be a legitimate way to earn passive income, but it's important to be careful. Make sure you're working with a reputable supplier and that you understand the risks involved.

By following these tips, you can help protect yourself from passive income scams and find legitimate opportunities to earn money.

Importance of Taking Action and Starting Small

Passive income can be a great way to earn extra money without having to put in a lot of effort. However, it's important to remember that creating passive income streams takes time and effort.

One of the most important things you can do is to take action and start small. By taking action and starting small, you can build momentum and create a solid foundation for your passive income streams.

Starting small allows you to test the waters and see what works and what doesn't. It also helps you to avoid taking on too much too soon. When you start small, you can focus on one or two passive income streams and give them the attention they need to be successful.

Another benefit of starting small is that it allows you to learn as you go. You can make mistakes and learn from them without risking too much. By learning from your mistakes, you can improve your passive income streams and make them more profitable in the long run.

One way to start small is to focus on low-cost passive income streams. For example, you could start a blog or a YouTube channel. These are low-cost ways to create passive income streams that can grow over time.

You could also consider investing in dividend-paying stocks or real estate investment trusts (REITs). These are relatively low-cost ways to create passive income streams that can provide steady income over time.

Remember, the key to creating successful passive income streams is to take action and start small. By doing so, you can build momentum, learn as you go, and create a solid foundation for your passive income streams.

So, don't wait any longer. Start taking action today and start building your passive income streams!

ABOUT THE AUTHOR

Dennis Snyder has been an entrepreneur all of his life. As a kid he began selling little homemade martini, olive stickers shaped like little sword. He didn't make a lot of money selling them but back then penny candy was actually a penny. He has five passive income assets at the moment and is working on number six. He is not wealthy but is financially free.